W9-CBJ-000

THE SECRETS
TO THE GAME OF
GOLF
& LIFE

Creative Director: Michael McKee

Art Direction & Design: Tim McGovern

Published by: Successories, Inc. (800) 621-1423

The Secrets To The Game Of Golf & Life
© Copyright 1997 Collins/Finkel LLC
ISBN #1-880461-41-2

This book is copyrighted material. All rights reserved. It is against the law to make copies of this
material without getting specific written permission in advance from Successories, Inc. No part of
this publication may be reproduced, stored in a retrieval system or transmitted in any form or by
any means electronic, mechanical, photocopying, recording or otherwise, without prior written
permission of the publisher. Printed in the United States of America.

THE SECRETS
TO THE GAME OF
GOLF
& LIFE

BY LEONARD FINKEL
PAINTINGS BY GARY MAX COLLINS

SUCCESSORIES LIBRARY

ACKNOWLEDGEMENTS

There are a multitude of people I would like to thank for making this book a reality, but the following deserve special recognition. Dr. Greg Gallick and Carolyn Dorfman, Mike Kutcher, Jack Finkel, Eric Freidman; The Doral Golf Resort, especially Jim McLean and Lani Collins, Buster Newton, John Collins, Peter Titlebaum, Harvey and Helen Penick, Tinsley Penick; the people at Successories, Jim Beltrame, Peter Walts, Michael McKee and Tim McGovern in particular; and most notably, Gary Max Collins, who first proposed the idea for this book and whose paintings make it special.

TABLE OF CONTENTS

FOREWORDS

Late one evening a few years back, I received a call from a friend I hadn't heard from in a while. It was Leonard Finkel calling to tell me he had experienced some changes in his outlook on life and business. He wanted to come back to Park City and spend some time with his golf game. Knowing Leonard's personality from previous experience, I was eager to meet the "New Leonard" and help him with his newfound enthusiasm for the game of golf.

That spring Leonard did show up with a refreshing new outlook on life. The changes came, in short, from a combination of teachings and philosophies. These boiled life down to some very simple concepts that were easier to understand and follow. Now it was time to apply this wisdom to his golf swing!

We started with some very basic skills that are critical to building a good foundation. I tried to emphasize the importance of understanding and practicing the fundamentals from which everything else grows. While these concepts are easy to practice, they are very difficult to master. Leonard, meanwhile, was very anxious to improve and felt like he should be spending more time on the complex aspects of the swing itself. We spent countless hours in my office trying to make sense of it all, and I think we both learned some great lessons in the process.

Leonard had been able to change his life by learning and understanding some basic principles and applying them. I approach my responsibilities as a teacher in the same manner. If we can build a strong foundation by understanding and patiently mastering the fundamentals, many of the complexities and difficulties of the swing — and of the game itself — simply disappear.

Mike Kutcher

MIKE KUTCHER
Director of Golf, Park Meadows Golf Club

This wonderful book of golf quotes, or quotes we can apply to golf, puts the game of golf into perspective.

I love how Leonard has organized the thoughts and ideas into a very simple format. The artwork by Gary Collins is simply outstanding.

There are great secrets to golf and more inside these covers. Read. Learn. Enjoy.

JIM MCLEAN
Director of Golf & Instruction, Doral Resort and Country Club

How thrilled my father, Harvey Penick, would be to know that Leonard Finkel's love and understanding of life and this great game of golf has been so eloquently and beautifully presented in his book, "The Secrets to the Game of Golf & Life."

During the last year of my father's life, Leonard made a pilgrimage to Texas for a visit. These two men, of different ages and backgrounds, became kindred spirits and soul brothers. Leonard has brought this special feeling to the pages of his new book. The wisdom gained through the ages of mankind – apply those principles to golf – my, how my dad would love this book! I think you will, too.

Tinsley Penick

TINSLEY PENICK

GOLF & LIFE

Golf has been my passion since I began playing seven years ago. Like millions of others, I was severely bitten by the bug. Some time ago, I realized something was missing from my golf game. To make a long story short, my desire to be the best golfer that I could be made me a better human being. It led me to the worlds of religion, philosophy, martial arts, and self-help. Through this journey I discovered that the lessons of life could be found in the pursuit of my passion...the game of golf. I am now able to enjoy the game that used to drive me and my fellow golfers crazy.

The underlying theme here is that the game of golf mirrors the game of life, and the lessons learned are interchangeable. They are about awareness, understanding, acceptance, and enjoyment...AWARENESS of the golfer you are and your current skill level... UNDERSTANDING why you are at that level and what is necessary for you to improve...ACCEPTANCE of what is and what will be...and the ENJOYMENT that results from following your passion.

Using brief thoughts matched with meaningful aspects of the game, I've written my own ideas and compiled them with insights from people in all walks of life. After a remarkable meeting with the versatile artist Gary Max Collins, my vision of this book began to crystallize. Gary's wonderful paintings blended perfectly with my vision, yet allowed for individual interpretation. This combination of art and thought seems to facilitate the digestion of individual concepts in a short period of time and may have its greatest impact in the chapter on visualization.

I suggest that you read this work in intervals. Give the ideas and images time to sink in. Then golf…reflect…live…and golf again. I hope you find that the lessons learned will enhance your golf and your life. Enjoy,

Leonard Finkel

L E O N A R D   F I N K E L

GOLF

golf as life · life as golf

"Golf is the toy department of life.
So it should be enjoyed."

Herb Graffis

"Golf is like fishing and hunting. What counts is
the companionship and fellowship of friends,
not what you catch or shoot."

George Archer

"It's believing that the results are so important
that also creates most of the misery I see on the
golf course. There is more to golf than the score.
I've felt it, and I know there must be others who
recognize that games are far more than results."

Timothy Gallwey

Red Cliffs & Verdant Greens

*"The person who enjoys his work as much as his hobby
is a genius. The golfer who lets frustration destroy
the pleasure of the game is a fool."*

ANONYMOUS

GOLF

golf as life · life as golf

"We pay so much attention to the bottom line, the scoreboard, our score, that we miss out on the 'game' itself. In golf as in life, it's not so much the scoreboard, but enjoying the journey that really counts. Don't miss it."

Leonard Finkel

"When you disappear – the thoughts, worries, and judgments you have about yourself – Golf as Art shows up. The resulting void is where all the important discoveries – the personal development, satisfaction, joy, and fulfillment – take place."

Fred Shoemaker

How Sweet It Is

"Like life, golf can be humbling. However, little good comes from brooding about mistakes we've made. The next shot, in golf or in life, is the big one."

GRANTLAND RICE

GOLF

"A golfer has to learn to enjoy the process of trying to improve.
That process, not the end result, enriches life."

Dr. Bob Rotella

"I believe that the real purpose of games is to develop skills
that will be useful in life, and golf is a perfect example."

Fred Shoemaker

"Golf is deceptively simple and endlessly complicated.
It satisfies the soul and frustrates the intellect. It is
at the same time rewarding and maddening – it is without
a doubt the greatest game mankind has ever invented."

Arnold Palmer

Timeless Terrain

"'Many people would enjoy such a view,' said the sage.
'They might aspire to make the climb and might desire
the satisfaction of standing here. But they didn't reach the top
or enjoy the view, and we are – not because we are smarter
or stronger or more deserving, but because we made the climb.
Only those who make the climb get to enjoy the summit.'"

DAN MILLMAN

GOLF

"...as ye grow in gowf, ye come to see the things
ye learn there in every other place. The grace that comes
from such a discipline, the extra feel in the hands, the
extra strength in knowin', all those special powers ye've
felt from time to time, begin to enter our lives."

Michael Murphy
"Golf in the Kingdom"

"The problem is that we confuse the goal of the game,
which is scoring as low as possible (winning), with the
purpose of the game, which we decide for ourselves.
This obsession with performance and winning dominates
all games in our society, not just golf."

Fred Shoemaker

Feeling The Flow

"*You will do foolish things, but do them with enthusiasm.*"
COLETTE

GOLF

golf as life · life as golf

"You can teach a student for that day, but if you can teach him to learn by creative curiosity, he will continue the learning process as long as he lives."

C. P. Bedford

"Golf would not be the game that it is without the continual hope of doing better the next time we play."

Mike Hebron

"There has always been something new, demanding, and testing every day I play. I love the challenge."

Nancy Lopez

Seize The Day

"Discovery is an ongoing, lifelong process."

LEONARD FINKEL

GOLF

golf as life · life as golf

"Golf is no different than life;
in difficult situations, perseverance will
ultimately produce character, which breeds success."
Bobby Clampett

"You are what you think you are, in golf and in life."
Raymond Floyd

"What we play is life."
Louis Armstrong

Hills And Dales

"Golf is life and life is golf. The lessons learned are interchangeable."

LEONARD FINKEL

"There are any number of people who have devoted enough thought, time, and effort to the game to become reasonably good, if they had only started out with an accurate conception of what to do."

Bobby Jones

"Perhaps analysis and the separate mastery of each element are required before the instincts are ready to assume command, but only at first. Command by instinct is swifter, subtler, deeper, more accurate, more in touch with reality than command by conscious mind. The discovery takes one's breath away."

Michael Novak

Next To Nature

"*Nature's way is simple and easy, but men prefer
what is intricate and artificial.*"

LAO TZU

"One reason golf is such an exasperating game is that
a thing learned is so easily forgotten, and we find ourselves
struggling year after year with faults we had discovered
and corrected time and again. But no correction seems
to have a permanent effect, and as soon as our minds
become busy with another part of the swing,
the old defect pops up again to annoy us."

Bobby Jones

"Golf is a game played by human beings. Therefore, it is
a game of mistakes. The best golfers strive to minimize
mistakes, but they don't expect to eliminate them. And they
understand that it's most important to respond well
to the mistakes they inevitably make."

Dr. Bob Rotella

Like A Walk In The Park

"Golf is not me versus my opponent. It is not me versus the course. Golf is me versus my thoughts."

LEONARD FINKEL

"Have realistic expectations and set attainable goals. Reaching intermittent, moderate goals is certainly more rewarding and enjoyable than floundering amid unrealistic expectations."

Leonard Finkel

"Maintain an attitude of unconditional self-worth, free from self-criticism. You can agree that it is cruel and unnecessary to tell someone else, 'You are really stupid – what a klutz – you should give up – you keep making the same mistakes – you'll never be any good!' If you would never say those things to anyone else, why not pay yourself the same courtesy?"

Dan Millman

"The price of success is hard work, dedication to the task at hand, and the determination that whether we win or lose, we have applied the best of ourselves to the task at hand."

Vince Lombardi

Up And Over

"Your chances of success in any undertaking can always be measured by your belief in yourself."

ROBERT COLLIER

"The swing is an action where certain things are caused
to happen and certain things are allowed to happen.
Faults arise in trying to cause what should be allowed."

Denise McCluggage

"Hitting a golf ball is an act so precise that there is
unlimited room for error. That error begins
in the mind and finds expression in the swing."

Lorne Rubenstein

"Letting go is ineffective unless it is preceded by both
physical conditioning and mental training. There is no
substitute for the hard work and self-discipline that go
into athletic training, but without the ability to let go,
the discipline invested can actually be counterproductive."

Dr. Gary Wiren

Anything's Possible

*"People fear letting go of control, but at some point
in a good golf swing, you must. The more important the shot,
the more difficult it is to give up control. Ironically, that's the
highest form of mental toughness – letting go of conscious control."*

DR. RICHARD COOP

AWARENESS
understanding

"Fear ruins more golf shots, for duffer and star,
than any other one factor."

Tommy Armour

"Courage is fear turned inside out. It is impossible
to be courageous if at first you weren't afraid."

Dr. Bob Rotella

"Fear closes the ears of the mind, and the terror we fear
is often empty. But nevertheless it causes real misery."

Freidrich Schiller

"To live a creative life, we must lose our fear of being wrong."

Joseph Chilton Pearce

I Love It

*"We tend to move to our comfort zones. To reach a goal,
we must expand a comfort zone."*

JAMES NEWMAN

"A leading difficulty with the average player is that he totally misunderstands what is meant by concentration. He may think that he is concentrating hard when he is merely worrying."

Robert Trent Jones

"We must come to understand that the very act of trying brings tension and rigidity. Once we understand how to learn, we will stop trying."

Mike Hebron

"By concentrating on precision, one arrives at technique; but by concentrating on technique, one does not arrive at precision."

Bruno Walter

Perfection

"What is concentration? It is not thinking or trying hard.
It is a relaxed awareness of the present situation, an
almost imperceptible, computer-like blending of variables,
producing a confidence, a very real belief, that what is
about to happen will unfold exactly as planned."

LEONARD FINKEL

AWARENESS
understanding

"Take care of the process;
the results will take care of themselves."
Leonard Finkel

"It goes without saying that as soon as one cherishes
the thought of winning the contest or displaying
one's skill in technique, swordsmanship is doomed."
Takano Shigeyoshi

"You don't get to control any outcome,
only every choice you make along the way."
Stephen Paul

Evening Shadows

*"Trying: When an archer is shooting for enjoyment, he has all his skill.
When he shoots for a brass buckle, he gets nervous. When he shoots
for a prize of gold, he begins to see two targets."*

C H U A N G   T Z U

"Thinking instead of acting is the number one disease in golf."

Sam Snead

"There is a part of all of us that wants to control things, do more, make things happen. But think about your own instances of extraordinary play and descriptions you've read of others'. Isn't the dominant experience one of not controlling, of trusting yourself and letting go?"

Fred Shoemaker

"Many times I have had fans tell me how cool I looked on the course, when all I could remember was how scared or nervous I had been."

Tom Kite

Evanescent

"When you can't think straight, don't think – feel."

LEONARD FINKEL

"This game will definetly make strong men cry."

Dave Marr

"If I had Jack's mind with my swing,
you might never have heard of Nicklaus."

Tom Weiskopf

"Putting is like genetics. I'm in the horse business,
so I've studied genetics for 25 years; and I've played golf
for a lot longer. And the conclusions I've reached about
putting and genetics are, number one, success is what works;
and number two, I know a lot about nothing."

Gary Player

A Round Of Pleasure

"If I'd have cleared the trees and driven the green,
it would have been a great tee shot."

SAM SNEAD

"My favorite shots are the practice swing and the conceded putt.
The rest can never be mastered."

Lord Robertson

"A golf course is a huge expanse of carefully prepared terrain...
It was not laid out so that balls could be hit into holes,
nor that a player could make a low score and feel good
about himself – in fact, the course is designed in many ways
to frustrate one's chances of low scores. The real purpose
for laying out the course is to provide certain benefits for the
golfer that transcend the mere mechanics of a golf game."

Timothy Gallwey

"People who talk about choking under pressure have no idea how
many things can go wrong on a golf course besides nerves and fear."

Arnold Palmer

Going With The Flow

*"Golf assuredly is a mystifying game. It would seem that, if a person
has hit a golf ball correctly a thousand times, he should be able
to duplicate the performance at will. But this certainly is not the case."*

BOBBY JONES

"I am convinced that the happiest and best golfers are those who have realized that there is no single gimmick that works, and that good golf is attained only by patience and humility, and by continually practicing both the outer and inner games."

Timothy Gallwey

"Practice is the only golf advice that is good for everybody."

Arnold Palmer

"The will to win is not nearly so important
as the will to prepare to win."

Bobby Knight

"Don't be too proud to take lessons. I'm not."

Jack Nicklaus

Precision

"Seek progress, not perfection. The perfect swing doesn't exist."

LEONARD FINKEL

"Did I learn anything from San Francisco? Well, just put me in the Open with a seven-stroke lead and nine holes to play again, and I promise that I won't let that opportunity slip by a second time."

Arnold Palmer

"Failure, more than success, is golf. Every great golfer at times has failed. Should we expect better?"

Leonard Finkel

"I think I fail a bit less than everyone else."

Jack Nicklaus

Heavenly Afternoon

"Good players are good because they come to wisdom through failure."

WILLIAM SAROYAN

"We tend to believe that our level of competence
is higher than it actually is. To improve, to be our best,
we must first accept who we truly are."
Leonard Finkel

"The most detrimental thing to effective practice
is an exaggerated belief in how good you are."
Dean Reinmuth

"You see, when you wish upon a star, it doesn't matter
who you are, but technique is everything. Positive thinking
is nice, but nowhere near as effective as truthful thinking."
Perry W. Huffington

Par For The Course

*"Realistic vision, a deep awareness of your potential
in a given endeavor, enables you to choose the wisest course
and to train for it. From a good beginning, all else flows."*

D A N   M I L L M A N

"Mistakes are essential to progress. The willingness
to learn from them is the backbone of any progress.
The object is to succeed, not to count your mistakes."

Tae Yun Kim

"As I get older, I try to think of the bad things
that happen to me on the golf course as 'tests.'
They're not hurdles; they're not bad marks or
punishments. They're things I need in my life,
things that bring me back to reality."

Frank Beard

Playing A Round

"*The world is so constructed that if you wish to enjoy its pleasures,*
you must also endure its pains. Whether you like it or not,
you cannot have one without the other."

SWAMI BRAHMANANDA

unexpected challenges
ACCEPTANCE

"Awareness of our strong points brings confidence, inspiration, motivation, and satisfaction. Only awareness of our weaknesses, however, allows us to strengthen our weak links and improve consistently. "

Dan Millman

"Step by step. I can't see any other way of accomplishing anything."

Michael Jordan

Timeless Pleasure

*"Don't go along with the crowd. Go your own way.
And practice, practice. Goddamnit, practice."*

BEN HOGAN

"Pressure is something every golfer feels at one time
or another...Sometimes when I putted, I looked like
a monkey trying to wrestle a football."

Sam Snead

"Of all games, golf exposes fraud
and self-delusion most efficiently."

Jim McLean

"At night, a golfer can program her mind with
great expectations. But she must throw them away
when she steps onto the first tee."

Dr. Bob Rotella

Starry Night

*"Golf is a compromise between what your ego wants you to do,
what experience tells you to do, and what your nerves let you do."*

BRUCE CRAMPTON

unexpected challenges
ACCEPTANCE

"Thanks to my new hearing aid, I can hear the click
of the club against the ball again. Unfortunately,
I heard it click 77 times today."

Arnold Palmer

"The average player has hit perfect shots and expects
that he always should. Yet the best players in the world
understand that it's simply not possible
to hit great shots all the time."

Leonard Finkel

Cloud Over Red Cliffs

*"Artists who seek perfection in everything
are those who cannot attain it in anything."*

EUGENE DELACROIX

"Golf puts a man's character on the anvil and his richest qualities – patience, poise, restraint – to the flame."

Billy Casper

"Few people realize that even the greatest of athletes have moments when they can feel the tension building up within themselves. The only difference between the great athletes and the duffer in relation to this phase of athletics is that the great athlete can recognize the signs of tension and take steps to correct them, because experience has taught him how to control this build-up within himself."

Sam Snead

"Courage is resistance to fear, mastery of fear, not absence of fear."

Mark Twain

High Plains Drifter

"In the process of confronting our fears, we overcome them."

LEONARD FINKEL

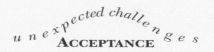

"I have always had a drive that pushed me
to try for perfection, and golf is a game in which
perfection stays just out of reach."

Betsy Rawls

"Our greatest glory is not in never falling,
but in rising every time we fall."

Confucious

"Let's face it – if you are an amateur player, you are not
going to be so accurate with a driver (or 3-wood)
that you can consistently place the ball in a certain
segment of the fairway. And let me tell you a secret:
most of the PGA tour pros aren't that accurate, either."

Butch Harmon

Dancing

"Only the mediocre are always at their best."

JEAN GIRAUDOUX

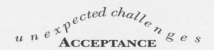

ACCEPTANCE

'You know, Tom, no matter how good you get at this game,
a lot of funky, crazy things are going to happen on the
golf course. The better you can get at accepting them,
the better you're going to get."

Dr. Bob Rotella to Tom Kite

"Expect trouble as an inevitable part of life,
and repeat to yourself the most comforting words of all:
This, too, shall pass."

Ann Landers

"Golf is not fair. Like life, it seems we get more bad breaks than
good. How we handle them is what matters."

Leonard Finkel

Against The Wind

"*All great players know there are days when,*
no matter what they do, the game wins."

DR. GARY WIREN & DR. RICHARD COOP

"The old proverb that it is necessary for a child to walk
before it runs is absolutely true on the links. At the
present time, one sees thousands of Golf Children
trying to run, when in reality they cannot walk."

G. S. Brown

"Golf and life are controlled by natural laws
that can't be changed. Accept it."

Leonard Finkel

Serenity

"*All that matters is if you can look in the mirror and honestly tell the person you see there that you've done your best.*"

JOHN MCKAY

"The inability to forget is infinitely more devastating
than the inability to remember."

Mark Twain

"Obstacles are what you see
when you take your eyes off your goal."

Anonymous

"The time between shots is a time to put the past
in the past, create a future that is powerful
and full of possibility, and live into the future."

Fred Shoemaker

The Calm Of The Green

"If you let cloudy water settle, it will become clear. If you let your cloudy mind settle, your course will also become clear."

BUDDHA

MENTAL FOCUS

"The place in which you find yourself isn't nearly as important as where you place your attention while you are there."

Stephen Paul

"It makes little difference what is actually happening; it's how you, personally, take it that really counts."

Dr. Denis Waitley

"A short debriefing session after every shot provides an opportunity to mentally reinforce favorable swing results – and to neutralize unfavorable ones. So, when you do produce a good shot, stay with it for a few seconds. Savor it, enjoy it, feel it. Re-experience it."

Dr. Gary Wiren & Dr. Richard Coop

On Course

"Focus on doing the right things in order to do things right."
LEONARD FINKEL

"I never blame myself when I'm not hitting. I just blame
the bat, and if it keeps up, I change bats. After all,
if I know that it isn't my fault that I'm not hitting,
how can I get mad at myself?"

Yogi Berra

"What people say to themselves about an experience,
their self-talk, often has more impact on their lives
than the experience itself."

Dr. Paul D. Ware

"Don't let what you cannot do interfere with what you can do."

John Wooden

Emerald Greens

*"Put your heart, mind, intellect, and soul even into your smallest acts.
This is the secret of success."*

SWAMI SIVANANDA

emotions emotions emotions

"You are either the captive or the captain of your thoughts.
You can resign yourself to mediocrity or you can
dare to dream of conquering outer space."

Dr. Denis Waitley

"Most golfers prepare for disaster.
A good golfer prepares for success."

Bob Toski

"Let our advance worrying become
advanced thinking and planning."

Sir Winston Churchill

Playing The Course

*"The correlation between thinking well and making successful shots
is not 100 percent. But the correlation between bad thinking
and unsuccessful shots is much higher."*

Dr. Bob Rotella

"The ability to concentrate is good, but thinking too much about how you are doing what you're doing is disastrous. Trust your muscles and hit the ball to the hole. Keep it simple."

Harvey Penick

"With mind clear, the body is at its peak efficiency and awareness. When you are in action, it's best to 'lose your mind and come to your senses.'"

Dan Millman

"I can't think and hit at the same time."

Yogi Berra

Effortless

"*The less effort, the faster and more powerful you will be.*"

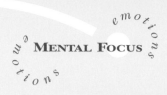

"It's not always a matter of whether you've got it or you don't, but whether you are willing to work at developing your emotional control. The first step is to understand that your emotions, chiefly trust and doubt, play a key role in determining the existence of tension, and tension is detrimental to performance."

Dean Reinmuth

"If there is doubt in your mind over a golf shot, How can your muscles know what they are expected to do?"

Harvey Penick

"The transition from chaos to order depends upon your achieving true inner calm."

The I Ching

Focus

"No matter what your skill level, a healthy attitude and relaxed focus will allow you to perform to your ability more often."

LEONARD FINKEL

"Never tell yourself you can't make a shot.
Remember, we are what we think we are."

Gary Player

"Indecision is a killer. Be confident with your choices.
Wrong decisions will produce better results
than no decision at all."

Leonard Finkel

"A buoyant, positive approach to the game
is as basic as a sound swing."

Tony Lema

Graceful Pleasure

"Those who believe they can and those who believe they can't are both right."

ANONYMOUS

POSITIVE ATTITUDE
playing the game

"What is genuinely lacking in people is that they do not believe.
You are able to obtain in life what your belief
will enable you to obtain."

Muhammad Ali

"Always assume that if things are going good,
they will only get better, and better, and better."

Leland T. Lewis

"Free will is the greatest gift anyone could have given us.
It means we can, in a real sense, control our own lives. On the
golf course, it means that a player can choose to think about his
ball flying true to the pin, or veering into the woods. She can choose
whether to think about making a putt or just getting it close."

Dr. Bob Rotella

The Mistress Of The Green

"In the long run, men hit only what they aim at. Therefore, though they should fail immediately, they had better aim at something high."

HENRY DAVID THOREAU

"Let it happen. Don't try to make it happen.
No advice I can give is more important."

Jim McLean

"There is one essential to the golf swing...
the ball must be hit."

Sir Walter Simpson

"That little white ball won't move until you hit it,
and there's nothing you can do after it has gone."

Babe Zaharias

Golf In The Desert

*"My reaction to anything that happens on the golf course is no reaction.
There are no birdies or bogies, no eagles or double bogies; there are
only numbers. If you can learn that, you can play this game."*

JIM COLBERT

"A golfer can't dictate what his opponents shoot.
He can't wave his arms or tackle a playing partner
who's getting ready to putt. But he can always
reach within himself to bring out the best
in his battle against the laws of physics and par."

Arnold Palmer

"Give me a lever long enough
And a prop strong enough.
I can single-handed move the world."

Archimedes

"While others may say, 'What if I fail?'
I think, 'What if I succeed?'"

Leonard Finkel

Mystic Morning

*"Things turn out best for the people who make the best
of the way things turn out."*

JOHN WOODEN

"When you miss a shot, never think of what you did wrong.
Come up to the next shot thinking of what you must do right...
The average expert player – if he's lucky – hits six, eight,
or ten real good shots a round. The rest are good misses."

Tommy Armour

"It's easy to say after a bad swing, 'Forget it and hit your
next shot.' Try doing it, really doing it. It works wonders."

Leonard Finkel

"To be aware of targets throughout your round of golf –
as opposed to being totally preoccupied with hitting the ball –
is a big step for a golfer. It's the difference between playing
golf and spending eighteen holes trying to make golf swings."

Jim McLean

Paradise

"It is nothing new or original to say that golf is played one stroke at a time. But it took me years to realize it."

BOBBY JONES

"Risk vs. Reward – Be aware of what your options are.
Understand the possible risks of a shot vs. the potential
for success. Make your decision and accept
the results of your choice."

Leonard Finkel

"Simple awareness leads to consistency and improvement."

Fred Shoemaker

"Trust it; feel it; believe it;
let it happen."

Leonard Finkel

Evening Round

"All of our dreams can come true...
if we have the courage to pursue them."

WALT DISNEY

"I've come to realize I perform best when my subconscious
mind plays the ball and my conscious or thinking mind
is otherwise occupied."

Al Geiberger

"Re-evaluate and review your game when practicing.
When playing, just let it happen. See pictures,
do not use words; recall feelings, do not explain."

Mike Hebron

"The truth of a thing is the feel of it, not the think of it."

Stanley Kubrick

Following The Game Plan

"The ball's got to stop somewhere.
It might as well be at the bottom of the hole."

LEE TREVINO

VISUALIZATION

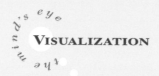

the mind's eye

"Golf is a target game: you aim for the fairway; you aim for the green; then you aim for the cup. Yet all too often amateurs hit ball after ball off the practice tee without visualizing at anything specific."

Curtis Strange

"I never hit a shot, even in practice, without having a very sharp, in-focus picture of it in my head. It's like a color movie. First, I see the ball where I want it to finish, nice, white, and setting up high on the bright green grass. Then the scene quickly changes, and I see the ball going there; its path, trajectory, and shape, even its behavior on landing. Then there's a sort of fade out, and the next scene shows me the kind of swing that will turn the previous images into reality."

Jack Nicklaus

Dead Solid Perfect

*"Visualize what you want to occur. Picture the perfect outcome.
Trust it. It will happen."*

LEONARD FINKEL

VISUALIZATION

the mind's eye

"From the tee box, the fairway looks so narrow.
Walk the same fairways at night and see how vast and wide
they really are. Picture that image at the tee box."

Leonard Finkel

"The mind contains all possibilities."

Buddha

"We use imagination to translate
theory into feeling."

Percy Boomer

Easy Does It

"Feel your swing. Picture the result."

LEONARD FINKEL

VISUALIZATION

the mind's eye

"By refusing failure, you are insuring success. You can brainwash yourself into seeing roses where the ground has been poisoned. Think positive, and positive things will happen to you."

Del Hessel

"I shut my eyes in order to see."

Paul Gauguin

"Let us train our mind to desire
what the situation demands."

Seneca

The Mind's Eye

"*Many more putts would go in if players credited holes with
a little of that catching power which they really possess.*"

S I R   W A L T E R   S I M P S O N

spirit of the game
ENJOYMENT

"Scenery seems to wear in one's consciousness
better than any other element in life."
William James

"When I get out on that green carpet called a fairway,
manage to poke the ball right down the middle,
my surroundings look like a touch of heaven on earth."
Jimmy Demaret

"Contemplating nature is one of the most obvious pleasures in golf.
Yet, it is often overlooked, especially by those so committed to
excellence and improvement that anything that does not directly relate
to their own game passes them by. If some of these self-ordained
Hogans gave in to a little casual bird-watching between shots instead
of brooding on their golf games, they'd probably play a lot better."
Dr. Gary Wiren & Dr. Richard Coop

Heaven On Earth

"What a beautiful place a golf course is. From the meanest country
pasture to the Pebble Beaches and St. Andrews of the world,
a golf course is to me a holy ground. I feel God in the trees and
grass and flowers, in the rabbits and the birds and the squirrels,
in the sky and the water. I feel that I am home."

HARVEY PENICK

spirit of the game

ENJOYMENT

"Hitting golf balls is meditation. It's like
running a vacuum cleaner through my mind
and removing any bad or annoying thoughts."
Mickey Wright

"Some of us worship in churches,
some in synagogues,
some on golf courses."
Adlai Stevenson

"Twas he wha taught me a' the graces o' the gemme,
to hold my temper when rereatin' from par and bogey,
to use the inner eye to make the game a very prayer."
Michael Murphy
"Golf in the Kingdom"

Blue Sky; Still Water

"All golfers, from high handicappers to experts, are creators
of their own commentaries of the game. Dreams, experiences,
tales of glory and woe, desire, love and death, reflection,
rapture – all these are among the commentary golfers bring
to the pro shop and onto the practice tee."

H A R V E Y   P E N I C K

ENJOYMENT

"A golfer is like an artist;
The sky is his canvas,
The ball is his paint, and
The club is his brush.
Each shot is a new painting."

Dean Reinmuth

"Use the talents you possess;
for the woods would be very silent
if no birds sang except the best."

Anonymous

Feel The Green

"What other people may find in poetry,
I find in the flight of a good drive."

A R N O L D   P A L M E R

spirit of the game

ENJOYMENT

"Golf is 20 percent mechanics and technique.
The other 80 percent is philosophy, humor,
tragedy, romance, melodrama, companionship,
camaraderie, cussedness, and conversation."

Grantland Rice

"Possibilities imply a free range of outcomes, any one of which
could occur. There will certainly always be outcomes that are more
desirable than others, but therein lies the Art of the Possible.
Becoming aware of the vast range of possibilities, and then
accepting with grace and maturity those that occur while still
keeping open the full range, requires skill, courage, and a spirit
of adventure. But it is indeed possible, and well worth it."

Fred Shoemaker

• *94* •

Balance Of Life

"Wherein an ordinary player learns that the course is the world, that the game is a process, and that, in order to 'win,' the person with the club must be no more and no less than a part of nature."

KJELL ENHAGER

spirit of the game

ENJOYMENT

"Age has thickened him, made him look almost muscle-bound,
and has grizzled his thin, untidy hair, but his deportment
more than ever expresses vitality, a love of life that returns
to him from the multitudes as fervent gratitude.
Like us golfing commoners, he risks looking bad
for the sake of some fun."

John Updike on Palmer

"One does not love a place the less
for having suffered in it."

Jane Austen

Purple Shadows On Green

"Being able to play in a beautiful setting is part of the essence of golf. When I'm on a course, I might be in the middle of one of the largest cities in the world with a six-lane superhighway nearby, but I have no sense of that. Instead, I'm in lovely surroundings, and that natural beauty is important to me."

ARNOLD PALMER

ENJOYMENT

"The challenge of accepting whatever lie we get is fundamental
to the pleasures of golf. To accept the rub of the green,
even when we must cross it against the grain, is to bring
an objectivity to our play that refreshes the spirit."

Coleman McCarthy

"I'd hate to see golf do what other sports have done.
I don't want the game to change. In fact, I'll go further
and say that one very important reason for golf's success
over the years is that the basic game hasn't changed."

Arnold Palmer

Blue, Green Or Gold

"Beyond the fact that it is a limitless arena for the full play of human nature, there is no sure accounting for golf's fascination...Perhaps it is nothing more than the best game man ever devised."

H E R B E R T   W A R R E N   W I N D

"Sure, it's possible to take golf too seriously,
but I don't see how people can do it for too long.
I mean, spending thousands of dollars and thousands
of hours to learn the best way to hit a little ball
into a little hole! Are you kidding? But of course,
it's also profound and magical, and we love it. It's perfect."

Fred Shoemaker

"To love what you do and feel that it matters...
how could anything be more fun?"

Katherine Graham

The Good Life

"A painting is never finished – it simply stops in interesting places."

PAUL GARDNER

FROM THE HEART OF A GOLFER
THROUGH THE EYES OF AN ARTIST

Gary Max Collins, born in 1936 has drawn and painted since early childhood. He attended BYU in the late '50s and the University of Utah in the early '60s. He has resided in Utah all his life, citing a deep love for the wide variety of natural settings which have provided such a rich source of inspiration for his paintings. Gary's personality is reflected in his avid style, both are likable, playful, articulate, and sensitive. His ability to transform an impression of scenic nature into a colorful freeze-frame on canvas excites even those who might normally reject contemporary art. In simple terms, a Gary Collins painting has been described as a place between what a landscape looks like and what it feels like. Collins explains that "He sees a scene, closes his eyes, fixes the picture in his mind and later in his studio, closes his eyes again and conjures up that scene." The result of this process is a painting that draws not only from the place the artist has seen, but also from a lifetime of colors, shapes and impressions. Gary Collins' paintings are an invitation to experience a place with him and see as only an artist can see.

Gary's recent passion for the game of golf has led him to explore and interpret the 'landscape' of the game as a reminder of the 'peace' he feels while on the golf course.

GARY MAX COLLINS